Life As ...

Life As a Spy in the American Revolution

Laura L. Sullivan

Cavendish Square

New York

Published in 2016 by Cavendish Square Publishing, LLC
243 5th Avenue, Suite 136, New York, NY 10016

Library of Congress Cataloging-in-Publication Data

Sullivan, Laura L., 1974-
Life as a spy in the American Revolution / Laura L. Sullivan.
pages cm. — (Life as...)
Includes index.
ISBN 978-1-5026-1081-2 (hardcover) ISBN 978-1-5026-1091-1 (paperback) ISBN 978-1-5026-1082-9 (ebook)
1. United States—History—Revolution, 1775-1783—Secret service—Juvenile literature. 2. Espionage—History—18th century—Juvenile literature. 3. Spies—History—18th century—Juvenile literature. I. Title.
E279.S85 2016
973.3'85—dc23

2015023782

Editorial Director: David McNamara
Editor: Kristen Susienka
Copy Editor: Nathan Heidelberger
Art Director: Jeffrey Talbot
Designer: Joseph Macri
Senior Production Manager: Jennifer Ryder-Talbot
Production Editor: Renni Johnson
Photo Research: J8 Media

The photographs in this book are used by permission and through the courtesy of: Sean Pathasema/Asher Brown Durand's The Capture of Major Andre.jpg/Wikimedia Commons, cover; John Parrot/Stocktrek Images/Getty Images, 5; Edward Gooch/Getty Images, 6; Public Domain/Library of Congress/Writing the Declaration of Independence 1776 cph.3g09904.jpg/Wikimedia Commons, 9; Library of Congress, 10, 12, 23; North Wind Picture Archives, 14; Otnaydur/Shutterstock.com, 15; J. Chereau/PrivateCollection/Bridgeman Images, 16; Hans F. Meier/iStock/Thinkstock, 19; Henry Clinton Papers, William L. Clements Library, The University of Michigan, 20; Science & Society Picture Library/Getty Images, 22; Public Domain/Benedict Arnold, Peggy Shippen Arnold/ArnoldCipherLetter.jpeg/Wikimedia Commons, 23; Public Domain/John D. Morris & Co. after painting by German artist Carl Wilhelm Anton Seiler/PreliminaryTreatyOfParisPainting.jpg/Wikimedia Commons, 24; KeanCollection/Getty Images, 27.

Printed in the United States of America

Contents

Introduction

Sometimes, wars are won by the most powerful side. Other times, though, wars are won by **intelligence**. Intelligence doesn't just mean being smart. It also means secret information that one government or group gathers to use against another. In a war, knowing about the enemy can help defeat them.

In the American Revolutionary War (1775–1783), spies played an important role in America's victory over the British. Some spies were military officers who snuck into enemy territory. Others were everyday people who watched ships, counted soldiers, and listened to gossip. Each played a part in helping to win the war.

George Washington, the commander in chief of the Continental Army, oversaw many spy networks during the American Revolution.

This illustration shows Patriots dressed like Native Americans destroying a tea shipment.

Chapter 1

The War for Independence

Since 1607, the American **colonies** had been under British rule. At first, most people were happy. The British provided trade, culture, and military support. As the colonies grew, though, many people began to dislike British rule. One main issue was **taxes**.

Britain taxed many things. If American colonists bought tea, paper, or ink, they paid a tax that went to Britain. Even worse, colonists had no say in the British government. Many colonists decided that America needed independence.

First, the colonists tried to tell Britain how they felt. The colonial government wrote letters to King George III, expressing their anger. When no agreement could be reached, it seemed like war was the only option. Fighting started in 1775 at the towns of Lexington and Concord in Massachusetts. Patriots formed their own government and wrote the Declaration of Independence in July 1776.

The British Army outnumbered the American forces. In 1776, the British captured New York. General George Washington, leader of the **Continental Army**, knew he had to take extraordinary measures to win the war. He began recruiting spies.

Patriots and Loyalists

People who wanted independence were called Patriots. Those who wanted America to remain under control of Britain were called Loyalists. Patriots and Loyalists might have been neighbors. There might even have been both Patriots and Loyalists in one family. This sometimes made spying easier. Unless a person said they supported a side, it was hard to tell what side someone was on.

Benjamin Franklin, John Adams, and Thomas Jefferson met to write the Declaration of Independence in 1776.

Colonel Benjamin Tallmadge was the leader of the Culper Spy Ring.

Chapter 2

Becoming a Spy

A spy system usually began in the army. An officer might contact Patriot friends and recruit them. It was dangerous work. If captured, spies might be hanged. If jailed, they could die of disease or starvation.

The War in Numbers

Population of the US in 1776 – About 2.5 million

Percentage of Patriots – About 40-45 percent

Percentage of Loyalists – About 15-20 percent

American soldiers killed in battle – About 6,824

British soldiers killed in battle – About 5,243

Total soldiers killed by disease or starvation (both sides) – 40,000-70,000 or more

Most spies were civilians—merchants, bakers, wives, or milkmaids. Often, they would swear loyalty and secrecy. In most cases, a spy only knew one or two other contacts. If one spy was captured, the rest of the spy system was still safe.

James Rivington was a well-known Loyalist newspaper publisher who was actually a Patriot spy.

New spies were sometimes given a cover, or a story that would explain their actions. For example, spies might pretend to be merchants or newspaper writers. That would give them an excuse to travel, take notes, or talk to people. Spies then memorized any special codes and learned secret writing styles.

Spy Girl

One of the earliest citizen spies was a young unnamed girl. Spymaster Benjamin Tallmadge, who reported directly to General George Washington, met with her. Pretending to sell eggs, she went into Philadelphia and received information about British troop movements. While reporting back to Tallmadge, they were attacked by the British. Tallmadge pulled her onto his horse and they rode into the night. The girl never showed fear, despite British gunfire. When they reached safety, she slipped away and was never discovered. Tallmadge and Washington were so impressed by her bravery that they decided to make more use of citizen spies.

A woman could sometimes get information from an enemy by acting as a gracious hostess.

Chapter 3

Life of a Spy

One of a spy's most important jobs was to not look like a spy. The best spies were often average citizens who paid attention and reported what they heard. A merchant working as a spy would spend a lot of time by the docks, supposedly meeting ships with goods to buy. At the same time, though, he was watching British ships. How many men were aboard? How many guns? Did the crew look ready to sail?

A spy would write down the information—often in code.

British troops landed at New York Harbor in 1776.

Later, a British officer might visit his store. While buying wine for a celebration, the British officer might mention that his troops planned to attack soon.

The merchant spy would either pass the information on to another spy or write it down. He would probably use a secret code, or maybe even invisible ink. The message could be kept in the spine of a book or hidden in a cloth-covered button. It might pass through two or three people before it reached the Continental Army.

A Day in the Life of a Female Spy

10 a.m.	Go shopping, gossip, observe troop movements
12 p.m.	Visit a friend whose cousin is a British officer; steal her letters from him
4 p.m.	Have tea with a Loyalist family, spread false information about a planned American attack to make the British send forces to the wrong place
8 p.m.	Dinner and dancing with British officers; give them wine to make them talkative
12 a.m.	Write coded letters in invisible ink for delivery in a **dead drop** the next morning

Women made good spies because they were often overlooked. A man traveling through occupied territory would probably be stopped and searched. A woman could say she was shopping or visiting a sick friend and might not be stopped.

One female spy is known only as Agent 355. She was part of a famous group known as the Culper Ring, a network of spies that worked for General Washington in New York. She was probably from a wealthy Loyalist family and got her information by flirting with British officers. Though she is credited with supplying Washington with some of the most important information, she probably died on a British prison ship after being captured.

Sometimes signals, such as using different colored laundry, were used to communicate with spies.

Sir W. Howe is gone to the Cheasapeak bay with the greatest part of the army. I hear he is landed but am not certain I am left to command here with too small a force to make any effectual diversion in your favour I shall try something at any rate. It may be of use to you. I own to you I think...

Spies hid their secrets in a "mask letter" that revealed a secret message when a special form was placed over the original letter.

Chapter 4

A Spy's Tools

Many people knew that writing with certain substances, such as onion juice, would produce an ink that was invisible until someone applied heat. This method was of little use to the Patriots because the British could easily reveal any hidden writing. The Patriots created a new kind of invisible writing.

Created by physician James Jay, brother of Patriot and Founding Father John Jay, this new kind of invisible ink could only be revealed by using a certain **solution**. Since the British didn't know the chemical process, Patriot secrets were safe. Letters using the "sympathetic stain" were written between lines of ordinary letters, or on pamphlets or books.

The *Turtle*

In 1775, Patriot David Bushnell invented the world's first attack submarine. He named it the *Turtle*. Made of wood in the shape of a clamshell, it was operated by one man. The *Turtle* was designed to attach explosives to the underside of British ships. It held enough air for about a half hour, and it could travel at about 3 miles per hour (4.8 kilometers per hour). Though it failed at its first mission and was sunk shortly after, its existence greatly worried the British.

For added safety, the messages might be written in code. Some codes were basic, where *A*=1, *B*=2, *C*=3, etc. They were easy to break. Other codes might have one word stand for another. If someone wrote that they expected delivery of ten loaves of bread on Wednesday, it might really mean that ten army squadrons were attacking on Wednesday.

Spy communication was often written in code, invisible ink, or both.

One popular code used books. Numbers would represent the page, the line, and the word's position in the line. Other people could only break the code if they had a copy of the same book.

Messages sent by ship were carried in tiny containers made of very thin metal. If capture was likely, they could be tossed overboard and sink. If thrown into a fire, they would melt. They could even be swallowed and found intact later.

In this code used by the Culper Ring, words were represented by numbers.

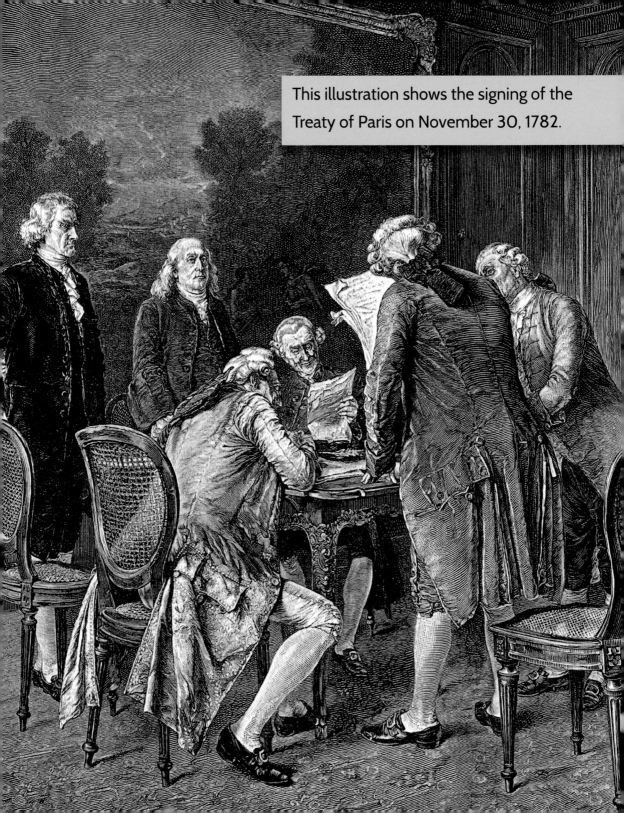
This illustration shows the signing of the Treaty of Paris on November 30, 1782.

Chapter 5

The Spies' Success

Patriot spies had many successes that helped win America's war for independence. The Culper Ring alone helped stop a British attack on French troops that had joined the American side. They stopped a British **counterfeiting** operation that would have made US money worthless. They even helped track down a traitor, Benedict Arnold, who had been an American major general before switching to the British side.

Major George Beckwith, a British intelligence officer, said, "Washington did not really outfight the British. He simply out-spied us." Spies helped a smaller, untrained army defeat one of the most powerful military forces of the era.

After the war, the United States continued to practice many of the same spy techniques. Today, computer codes have replaced handwritten messages. Modern submarines can stay underwater for more than ninety days, much longer than the *Turtle*'s thirty minutes. However, the basis of spying was–and still is–loyal, brave men and women willing to take risks to get information for their country.

The colonists had their own money.

This is $4 in Continental money.

Glossary

colonies Land, such as a country, governed by another country or nation.

Continental Army The American army during the Revolutionary War.

counterfeit False money made to replace real money; any imitation of something of value meant to deceive.

dead drop A method of leaving something in a secret location for another person to pick up.

intelligence Information collected, often in secret, used to help a nation, government, or military.

solution A liquid made with chemicals.

tax A percentage of income, or a percentage of the cost of purchased goods, collected by the government for its own use.

Find Out More

Books

Herbert, Janis. *The American Revolution for Kids: A History with 21 Activities*. Chicago: Chicago Review Press, 2002.

Platt, Richard. *Spy*. DK Eyewitness Books. New York: DK Children, 2009.

Schanzer, Rosalyn. *George vs. George: The American Revolution as Seen from Both Sides*. Des Moines, IA: National Geographic Children's Books, 2007.

Website

George Washington's Mount Vernon and His Spy Ring
www.mountvernon.org/george-washington/the-revolutionary-war/george-washington-spymaster

Video

Liberty's Kids: The Complete Series. Shout! Factory, 2008.

Index

Page numbers in **boldface** are illustrations. Entries in **boldface** are glossary terms.

About the Author

Laura L. Sullivan is the author of more than thirty fiction and nonfiction books for children, including the fantasies *Under the Green Hill* and *Guardian of the Green Hill*. She has written many books for Cavendish Square, including *Life As a Cowboy in the American West* and *Life As an Explorer with Lewis and Clark*. Or, she might really be a spy, and writing books for kids is just her cover …